SRAonline.com

McGraw Hill SRA

Printed in the United States of America.

Send all inquiries to:
SRA/McGraw-Hill
4400 Easton Commons
Columbus, OH 43219-6188

ISBN 978-0-07-612255-4
MHID 0-07-612255-7

11 12 13 14 MER 26 25 24 23

The McGraw-Hill Companies

The Princess and the Pea

by Hans Christian Andersen

Adapted by Susan Blackaby
Illustrated by Charlene DeLage

Reading Advisors:
Adria F. Klein, Ph.D.
Professor Emeritus, California State University
San Bernardino, California

Kathy Baxter, M.A.
Former Coordinator of Children's Services
Anoka County (Minnesota) Library

Susan Kesserlring, M.A.
Literacy Educator
Rosemount-Apple Valley-Eagan (Minnesota) School District

McGraw Hill SRA

Columbus, OH

Once upon a time, a noble king and a wise queen had a son. He was a fine young prince.

When it came time for the prince to marry, he had to find a wife.

“I can’t marry just any old princess,” said the prince. “I have to find a *real* princess.”

The prince traveled from place to place. He met many, many princesses.

All of them were very nice.
But the prince could not tell which of them were real princesses.
None of them seemed quite right.

The prince looked and looked and looked and *looked.* He looked all over the world, with no luck at all.

The prince was very sad.

“I’d like to marry a real princess,”

he said. “But I can’t find one!”

One winter night
a huge storm blew in.

Thunder boomed. Lighting flashed.

It rained like crazy!

Suddenly, there came a knock at the castle gate. It barely could be heard above the storm. "Who's there?" asked the king.

“A princess,” said a sweet voice.

“A princess!” the king exclaimed.

He opened the gate at once.

There stood a wet, muddy girl.

Her hair streamed like seaweed.

Her clothes were soaked.

Water flowed out of her shoes.

“Oh my! Look at this poor princess!” said the king.

“Are you a real princess?” asked the prince.

"Of course I am," said the princess.

"I'm just a bit messy."

“I’m not so sure she’s real,” thought the queen. “But I know just how to find out.”

The queen sneaked off to the bedroom. She removed all of the bedding. Then she put a green pea on the bed.

The queen put 20 mattresses on top of the pea. Then she put 20 feather beds on top of the mattresses.

The queen returned to the princess.
"Your bedroom is all set," she said.
"Thank you," said the tired princess.

The princess climbed up into bed.

“Sleep tight!” said the queen.

In the morning, the princess came down to breakfast. She greeted the king and queen.

"How did you sleep?" asked the queen.

"Bad, bad, bad!" said the princess.

"I didn't close my eyes. I tossed and turned all night! There was a bump in my bed."

"It was as hard as a rock!

It was as big as an elephant!

I'm black-and-blue all over!

I feel horrible!"

"How delightful!" said the queen. "Only a real princess would feel a little pea through all that fluff."

The prince was thrilled.
"I have found my real princess at last!" he said.

The prince and the princess were married the next day.

The pea was placed on display

in the royal hall.

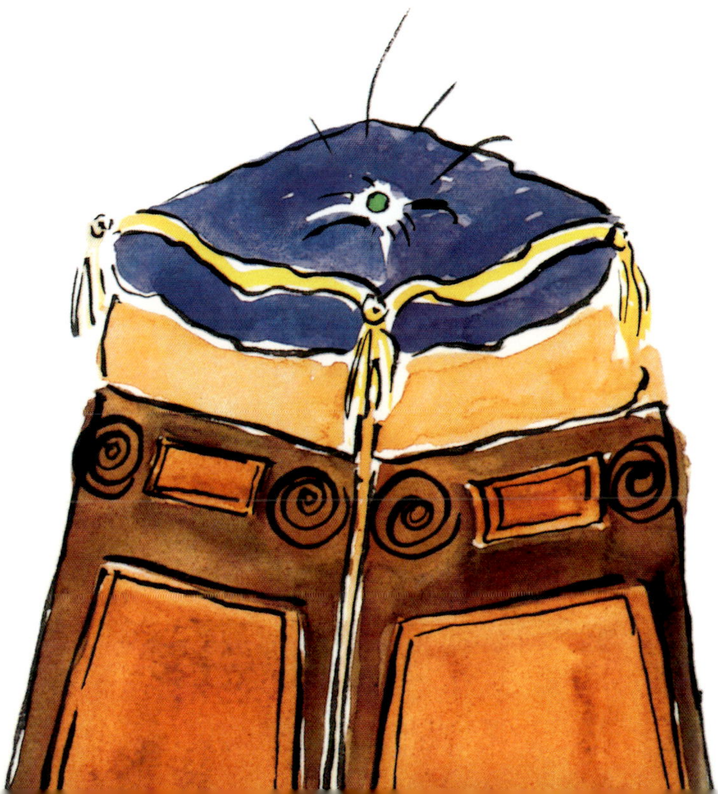